Roberto

PISA

ART AND
HISTORY

Published and printed by

plurigraf

NARNI - TERNI

INDEX

Index

© Copyright by Casa Editrice Plurigraf
S.S. Flaminia, km 90 - 05035 Narni - Terni - Italia
Tel. 0744 / 715946 - Fax 0744 / 722540 - (Italy country code: +39)
All rights reserved. No Part of this publication may be reproduced.
Printed: 1999 - Plurigraf S.p.A. - Narni

HISTORICAL OUTLINE

The name of the city is undoubtedly very ancient: through the millennia, right from the period of its foundation by the Ibero-Ligurians, it remained unchanged, whereas another Pisa in the Mediterranean later changed its name to Olympia for reasons of cult. Pisa is so named because it is situated at the confluence of two rivers, the Arno and the Serchio, Just as the ancient Greek Pisa had been founded in the delta between the Alpheus and the Cladeus. The name thus signifies meadowland or delta; the Arno and the Serchio, before they join, delimit an extensive area of marshland by which the city is isolated and defended.

Pisa, which is Europe's most ancient maritime city, always kept alive the Ibero-Ligurian name given it by its founders, its situation determined its destiny. The waterways it controlled made it a commercial emporium, and its inhabitants were ready to take to arms to defend its trade. Hence, the Etruscans did not advance beyond Volterra, while Pisa accepted Roman subjection with good grace because Rome, by weakening the Liguri-Apuani, provided it with a hinterland safe from threats and dangers. Under Roman rule the city prospered: it became embellished with temples and palaces, in the most sumptuous of which the emperors Hadrian and Antoninus Pius resided.

In the Middle Ages Pisa became a flourishing maritime trading centre and, at the time of the Investiture Contest, won contol as a free commune, reaching the height of its power in the vast

movement of struggle between the Christian world and the Islamic world constituted by the Crusades. At sea, by its daring enterprises in Sardinia, Corsica and Palestine, Pisa reinforced its power, and distinguished itself in the task of defending the Tyrrhenian from Barbar incursions.

After a long period of abandonment, Pisa enjoyed a period of revival under the rule of the Medici, who embellished the city with streets and palaces, reopened the ancient University (the Studio) and founded the Palazzo della Sapienza, which is today the seat of the University of Pisa.

In 1737, on the extinction of the Medici regime, the dynasty of Lorraine also showed a growing interest in the University, which was frequented by illustrious teachers and which increasingly became the main focus of civic life. Even during the Napoleonic period Pisa, on succumbing to French rule without resistance, maintained its primacy in Tuscany as a centre of higher studies; the University was turned into an Imperial Academy dependent on the University of Paris, and the Scuola Normale (university college) was founded. After the restoration, the city was restored to the House of Lorraine. Despite widespread adhesion to the reformist and paternalist regime of the House of Lorraine, however, the ideals of the Risorgimento continued to grow, especially among students; this led to the historic episode of the volunteers of the University of Pisa flocking to Garibaldi's standard and fighting at Curtatone and Montanara (1848). On the accession of Tuscany to the Kingdom of Italy, Pisa continued its cultural tradition which has been accompanied by some modest industrial growth, stimulated by the vicinity of Livorno.

The Arts: Architecture

Pisan art expressed its highest values in the architecture of the Romanesque period, in sculpture between 1260 and 1310 and in the painting of the 14th century. Buscheto (or Buschetto), whose name is inseparably linked with the Cathedral, opens the great chapter of the architecture of Pisa. Rainaldo, who continued Buscheto's work and began the façade of the Cathedral consecrated in 1118, is another great Pisan architect. The heritage of Buscheto and Rainaldo was bequeathed, in turn, to Dio-

tisalvi. The world-famous Leaning Tower, in fact the Bell-Tower of the Cathedral, was begun in 1173 and, according to a reliable tradition, is attributable to the Pisan architect Bonannus. Giovanni di Simone was also responsibile for the architecture of the Monumental Camposanto (or cemetery) of Pisa.

Though it was especially in sculpture that the pioneering creative personality of Giovanni Pisano distinguished itself, it should not be forgotten that he and his followers closed the most important period of Pisan architecture by the lower storey of the façade of Siena Cathedral and the façades of Santa Caterina and San Michele in Borgo in Pisa. Dating to the mid-12th century is also the foundation of the great circuit of town walls, which were erected to counter the threat posed by Frederick Barbarossa, and gave the city a unified architectural character.

Today the most important stretch is that of the walls of San Zeno, from which it is possible to ascertain that they were built in three phases and raised to their present level in a period attributable to the 14th century.

Sculpture

The development of Pisan sculpture in the Middle Ages is inseparably linked with that of architecture. Its initial characteristic was imitative fidelity to elements of the classical period for ornamental purposes. Between approximately 1120 and 1145, the lower storey of the façade of the Cathedral) was decorated with sculpture by unknown masters, who already attest to a flourishing cultural tradition.

Yet it was Guglielmo (buried, like Buscheto, in the façade of the Cathedral) who was the first

Historical outline

5

major personality of Pisan sculpture. Closely linked with the sylistic canons of Guglielmo were Gruamonte (active in Pistoia) and Biduino, who contributed to the decoration of the façade of the Cathedral prior to 1170. Bonannus, the builder of the Leaning Tower, also absorbed elements of Guglielmo's figurative culture which he expressed in his masterpiece: the side entrance to the Cathedral of Pisa, Nicola Pisano erupted onto the scene not only of Pisan, but European, sculpture with an undoubted masterpiece: the Pulpit in the Baptistery, sculpted in 1260. Prior to this work, Nicola Pisano, according to recent hypotheses, sculpted two high reliefs with the Nativity and the Deposition in the portico of the Cathedral of Lucca, where his presence in 1258 is certainly documented.

Subsequently, between 1266 and 1268, with the collaboration of his son Giovanni and Arnolfo di Cambio, he worked on the even richer and magnificent pulpit in the Cathedral of Siena. Nicola died, probably in Pisa, shortly before 1284.

Among his followers we find Arnolfo di Cambio and Nicola's own son, Giovanni Pisano, he too a very powerful personality as a sculptor and, what is more important, with a dramatic originality and a vigour all of his own which distinguish him from his father with whom he worked right up to the latter's death. An-

other important figure in the development of medieval Pisan sculpture was the Sienese Tino di Camaino, who was present in Pisa from 1310 to 1315 and who sculpted a baptismal font for the Cathedral, the marble altar-piece for the ancient altar of San Ranieri and the Tomb of Henry VII of Luxemburg, now in the Cathedral Museum.

Painting

The precedents which especially concurred to the formation of a Pisan pictorial tradition were, on the one hand, the school of Lucca (already flourishing in the mid 12th century) and, on the other, the work of the monastic "Scriptoria" in Lucca and Florence during the 11th and 12th century.

Giunta Capitini, known as Giunta Pisano, was the dominant personality in Pisan painting in the early 13th century.

The Crucifix in the church of San Ranierino at Pisa is his. With the anonymous Master of San Martino (so called on account of the Madonna and Child Enthroned from the church of San Martino attributed to him), the cycle of Pisan medieval painting draws to a close (7th-8th decade of the 13th century).

The most prestigious name among the foreign artists active in Pisa was, however, Masaccio, who painted a great polyptych for the church of the Carmine in 1426. This was unfortunately dismembered and dispersed in the 18th century.

Another great Florentine painter, Benozzo Gozzoli was also active in Pisa from 1468 to 1485, frescoing the Camposanto with Biblical Stories, which are unfortunately very damaged today.

The Magic Gate of Santa Maria suddenly reveals to our gaze, beyond the circuit of medieval walls, the emerald lawns on which stand the gleaming marble buildings of the Piazza dei Miracoli (as the Cathedral precinct is called).

There, before us, against its green backcloth, is the massive cylindrical bulk of the Baptistery; its delicate filagree of little arches and columns, pinnacles, cusps and statuettes creates a fantastic play of light and shade round its great cupola towering into the sky.

And there beside it are the marble Cathedral, a dazzling white casket, perfect in its equilibrium, and the robust Leaning Tower with its slender spiralling galleries and arcades. The Camposanto (or cemetery) completes this wonderful scene.

The blind arches along its unadorned walls repeat the characteristic architectural motif of the whole of the Piazza dei Miracoli, which, despite being the product of three centuries of building, constitutes a perfect ensemble and an unique achievement in the history of italian art: the expression of an original sensibility and a well-defined taste which takes the name of the Pisan-Romanesque style.

A further feature of this complex is that its monuments are arranged in an harmonious composition which represents the journey of faith of the believer: the Baptistery in which he was born to the faith; the Church in which he celebrates it; the Camposanto in which he will await the Resurrection; and the Bell Tower which symbolizes the impulse towards the divine.

It is from this point, that we will begin the first of our itineraries in our tour of the city and its most important monuments.

THE GATE OF SANTA MARIA

The magic gate of Santa Maria suddenly reveals to us, beyond the medieval walls, the green garden, where the marble architecture of Piazza dei Miracoli (the Square of Miracles) superbly rise. They stand there, as if they were suspended an ideal, poetical dimension out of time and the city area. Here is, on the deep green of the meadow, the cylindrical and massive structure of the Baptistery. The extremely delicate lace of small arches, columns, pinnacles, spires and statues creates a fantastic play of lights and shadows around the dome rising towards the sky.

And there it is, before it, that white jewel of balance, the marble Cathedral and the Leanirig Tower, slender in its round dance of loggias and arches.

The church-yard completes the wonderful scenery, whose blind arches of the simple walls take up the characteristic architectonic motif of the whole Piazza dei Miracoli. It is a monumental structure which, realized during three centuries, constitues a unique phenomenon in the history of the Italian art, a result of an original sensibility and clear taste, which is called Romanesque-Pisan style.

THE BAPTISTERY

The Baptistery was built with various interruptions, during a long period that extends from 1153, the year that it was begun by the architect Diotisalvi, to the end of the following century. Despite the fact that the original project was not faithfully followed, due to the succession of numerous artists and to the new architectural currents, the structure remains essentially Romanesque. A large part of the rich sculptural decoration of the upper stories can be attributed to Nicola and Giovanni Pisano whose original works, including statues of humans and animals, heads, bust of saints and prophets, have been substituted with copies in an effort to prevent their destruction.

INTERIOR

In the centre of the temple, on three steps, there is the Baptismal Font, whose severe and essential line is enriched with the polychromatic tarsias of the panels. Meant for baptism by immersion, once a more common rite, it consists of a large octagonal basin with other four smaller basins in the inside.

The Font was made in 1246 by Guido Bigarelli of Como. In the centre, a column with an Arab capital supports the statue of the Baptist, one of Italo Griselli's works. The particular acoustics of the building creates a very suggestive multiple echo which, like a large choir, repeats many times, under the ample vault, any sound or song.

Realized in 1260 by Nicola Pisano, this pulpit is not only a work of sculpture but also an architectural element in itself. In fact, it differs from the traditional wall supported pulpits and stands isolated on seven columns, some placed on the backs of lions and the central one resting on a base sculptured with figures of animals and gnomes.

The pulpit is hexagonal and enclosed on five sides by marble panels with high reliefs representing the Adoration of the Magi, the Presentation in the Temple, the Crucifixion and the Final Judgement. On the capitals, intercalated with trilobated arches, there are represented Faith, Charity, Strength, Humility, Faithfulness and Innocence.

THE CATHEDRAL

The Cathedral (Duomo) was erected by the Pisans following the victorious battles fought against the Saracens of the Mediterranean islands.

The construction was begun in 1063 by Buscheto whose tomb is awalled under the first arcade on the left side of the façade. In 1118, when the design of this great Pisan architect had been for the most part carried out, the Cathedral was consecrated by Pope Gelasius II.

After the death of its initiator, the construction suffered a set-back due to its inevitable tie to the economic resources of the Pisan Republic, to the changing of taste, and to the vicissitudes that occurred in over a century of history.

When work was resumed, some important modifications were brought to the original plan; the naves were lengthened, the transept was enlarged and the façade was built by the architects Rainaldo, successor to Buscheto, and Master Guglielmo, who also sculpted the first pulpit in the Duomo.

The Cathedral was built during the powerful maritime Republic's most flourishing period of political and economic expansion which reached its apex in an era characterized by a great exchange of political, economic, cultural and artistic interests among the soldiers, mercenaries and pilgrims who, in great numbers, were sailing to far off Eastern shores.

One can therefore understand the presence in Buscheto's architecture of Arab and Byzantine elements that, together with classi-

cal and Lombard characteristics inherited from the historical and cultural traditions of Tuscany, he so ably combined in this work, giving life to one of the most original creations of Italian Romanesque style. The actual plan

of the Duomo is in the form of a Latin cross, and the space of the interior, divided by classical colonnades into five naves in the longitudinal wing, and three in the transept, reflects the large Paleochristian construction that Buscheto studied during his documented trip to Rome. Exterior: On the sides, the high and light blind arches placed on pilasters of the lower part, the accelerated play of pilasters with lintels in the middle, and the arches that divide the elevation of the central nave, similar to those of the bottom section, are animated by coffered rhomb and rosette decorations, typical motives found in the most refined cathedrals of Asia Minor, by marble intarsia work and rich Eastern

influenced mosaics. On the tran-
cept crossing is an elliptical
dome placed on an octagonal
drum whose size is diminished
because of the graceful Gothic
marble decoration that was
added in 1380. In the lower part
of the façade Rainaldo repeated
the blind arch motif of the sides
on which he placed four orders
of arcades which form open galleries, graded according to the
inclination of the internal naves,
and graceful mullioned windows. This imposing Cathedral,
although it contains Lombard,
classical and oriental influences
and tendencies, asserts itself in
Italian art history as the basis of
a new and original language,
from which Pisan-romanesque
architecture gets its start.

INTERIOR

The interior has a spaciousness and classicism of forms of Paleo - christian inspiration which is animated by a new and modern style. The large arcades, supported by the closely placed colonnades, the proportions of the construction and the presence of the pointed triumphal arch give it a sense of vertical-

ism which is balanced, in the rhythmic layout of various architectural elements such as the projecting abacus on the capitals of the slender granite columns and the sharp cornice that separates the arcades and the loggias.

The upper order of arcades of the central nave, with the added pictorial accent afforded by the green and white horizontal marble band on the pilaster, repeats the division of space of the lateral naves, abouding numeros arches, vaults, crossvaults and columns.

THE PULPIT

The most valuable work of art in the Duomo is the Pulpit by Giovanni Pisano, done by the master in the first decade of the 14th century, dismantled after the fire of 1595 and recently recomposed. In this pulpit, monumental testimony to the dramatic art of Giovanni Pisano, every architectural element becomes a work of sculptures: from the caryatids representing St. Michael, the Evangelists, Hercules and the 4 Cardinal Virtues, and the figures of the Theological Virtues on the central pillar, to the Sibyls the magnificent panels. The Pulpit, enlivened by the excited movement of the forms, presents a continuous plastic development which is accentuated by the curved shape of the marble panels in which the Stories of Christ are narrated.

PANELS OF THE PULPIT

In the nine panels that enclose the upper part of the Pulpit, the stories of the life of Christ, form the Annunciation to the Crucifixion, are illustrated in an intense and implacable rhythm. The last two panels represent the Final Judgement: in one, the blessed and in the other, the damned. A feverish and disturbing anxiety can be detected in all the compositions, even in those with serene subject like the Nativity or with more idyllic contents like the Adoration of the Magi. In dramatic scenes such as the Slaughter of the Innocents, the Crucifixion, and the damned of the Final Judgement the artist hits on desperately tragic notes, in which the unrestrained rhythm of the lines dominates and accentuates the agitation of the compositions.

Pages 30-31: The Crucifixion Giovanni Pisano.

FAÇADE DOORS

The three bronze doors that open on the Cathedral façade are not the original ones by Bonannus since those had been lost in the fire of 1595 which also destroyed the ceiling and numerous frescoes. The actual doors were made in 1601 by artists from Giambologna's school including Pietro Tacca, Giovan Battista Caccini and Orazio Mochi, following designs made by Raffaello Pagni. The central door is flanked by two classical columns on which acanthus leaves are sculpted. The Stories of the Virgin are represented in a rich frame of human and animal heads and floreal motives.

THE DOOR OF ST. RANIERI (PORTA SAN RANIERI)

In the wing of the transept, facing the campanile, is the door of St. Ranieri, regular entrance to the Duomo.

The bronze panels, with scenes from the life of Christ, were made toward the end of the 12th century by Bonannus Pisano, whose refined art shows Hellenistic and Byzantine influences one in a new and original manner. The small, slender, picturesque figures are animated by an extraordinary liveliness obtained through the use of graceful, undulating lines and the skillful distribution of light and shade.

THE LEANING TOWER

The most distinctive monument in the Piazza dei Miracoli is undoubtedly the Leaning Tower. It was begun in 1173 by Bonanno, who ingeniously adopted the motif of the superimposed galleries used on Rinaldo's Cathedral façade. On reaching only its third storey, the building of the Tower had, however, to be abandoned due to a subsidence of the soil which caused its characteristic lean. The work was resumed a century later by Giovanni di Simone, who tried to rectify the Tower's inclination and raised it as far as its sixth storey. Cylindrical in structure, the Tower is surrounded by columned arcades: below, following the decorative scheme already used in the apse of the Cathedral, it consists of an order of tall blind arcades resting on semi-columns, with tiers of columns on round arches forming six open galleries rising above. A spiral staircase of 294 steps, running round the cylindrical core of the Tower, leads up to the top. Here is situated the bell-tower built by Tommaso, son of Andrea Pisano, in the mid-14th century. Of lesser diameter, the chamber consists of an elegant arcading resting on brackets and colonnettes which frame the various apertures. The seven bells placed inside the chamber are tuned according to the seven notes of the musical scale.

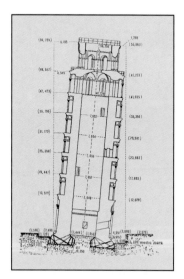

THE RENOVATION OF THE LEANING TOWER OF PISA

On 6th January 1990, it became necessary to close off access to the tower to the general public. Since then various Bills have appeared and subsequent interventions, agreed upon by a Committee of Experts appointed by the Prime Minister's Office - after a proposal by the Ministry for the Cultural Heritage and Environment and by the Ministry of Public Works -,have been carried out on the Tower to reduce its slant and slow down the monument's leaning process. Here are some of the most interesting. In the spring of '92 fears for the Tower's internal structural collapse led to its being "hooped": some 600 tons of lead ingots were positioned around its base on the opposite side to the potential collapse. At the end of '93 given the unsuccessful outcome of this intervention, an electroosmosis process was carried out on the Tower's foundation. After just a few months the latter project was abandoned as being ineffective. June '94 to June '95 saw the preliminary works for the subsequent application of 10 anchors vertical to the ground which were supposed to act as a counterbalance: the surroundig ground was "frozen" with liquid nitrogen.

However, in mid-September '95, the Tower began to move once more, but this time on the opposite side. Interventions were suspended and between '96 and '97 a solution was proposed to "anchor" the Tower to an external structure and to a subsequent excavation of the surroundig ground to reduce its leanig. In the summer of '98 horiwontal stays were installed, leading from the Tower to the "structure", which were supposed to stabilise is slant. In '99 the Tower should begin to lean less, thanks to the above-mentioned sub-excavation, thereby restoring to the people of Pisa and to the whole world the stability of this monument.

THE MONUMENTAL CHURCH-YARD

The Monumental Camposanto (cemetery), a unique architectural complex, rose at the end of the 13th century on the site where, tradition says, Archbishop Ubaldo Lanfranchi deposited earth from Calvary which had been brought back from a Crusade aboard Pisan ships. The construction was begun by Giovanni di Simone, and completed in the successive centuries. It consists of a long rectangular portico that encircles an ample green area, closed on the exterior by a marble enclosure with frescoes; a grandiose cycle in which all the Cristian tradition and Medieval mystical vision is reflected. Funeral monuments and chapels were built throughout the centuries while numerous ancient sarcophagi, classical and medieval statues and sculptures that are now scattered around Pisa, enriched the ample portico. Thus, this illustrious cemetery became a valuable artistic patrimony, with famous paintings and an important museum of classical sculpture, enclosed in a magnificent architectural monument.

Unfortunately the cemetery was tragically devastated during the last war by a fire provoked by a grenade; the frescoes remained

The Monumental Church-yard: The western passage.

altered and swollen because of the high temperature and the melting of the lead roof covering, and many of the sculptures were damaged or shattered. Thanks to the invaluable intervention of the Opera of the Primaziale and to the patient work of numerous experts, today it is possible to admire the completely restored sculptures, and the frescos, which had been removed from the walls using a complicated and delicate technique, restored and then recomposed, although with parts missing and colors altered. Also, when the paintings were taken off the walls, the preparatory sketches called synopses, over which the frescoes are painted, came to light, and these constitute not only a precious discovery but also a valid aid in the study of these masterpieces.

41

FRESCOES AND "SINOPIAS"

The most precious artistic patrimony of the Monumental Church-yard of Pisa is certainly represented by the magnificent cycles of frescoes which adorned its walls. During the 14th and 15th centuries famous artists, such as called "The Master of the Triumph of Death", decorated the Church-yard. If was so that the animated and terrible allegories of the Triumph of Death, the last Judgement, Hell and the fantastic cycles of the Stories of St. Ranieri and the St. Efisio and Potito of the Old

Testament came into being. Surprisingly preserved from the ravages of war, most of these frescoes are now exhibited in appropriate halls. A particular technique, rightly called "a strappo" (by pulls), having been used to restore them, the sketches and designs the artists used to make before colouring, which was carried on by their pupils, have come to light. These designs, which were realized by using a brush with a reddish earth called "sinopia", reveal the hand of the master and a surprising vividness. This is the reason why the "sinopias" and paintings of the Pisan Church-yard have always drawn the attention of critics and scholars. For it is very interesting, even for the ignorant, to compare the finished fresco with its sinopia.

THE TRIUMPH OF DEATH, THE CAVALCADE

The large composition is divided into various scenes: in the center is Death, who directs his scythe toward a group of young men and women gathered beneath a grove, while below the unhappy invoke him and, in the sky, the angels and demons contend the souls of the dead.

Above left, an example of the hermits who pass their lives away in solitude and prayer a party of riders about the fragility of earthly things while showing them the open graves containing the bodies of three kings in different stages of decay.

*The Final
Judgement.
A typical Medieval
representation of the
Final Judgement
that Vasari attri-
butes to Andrea
Orcagna: above,
Christ and the Ma-
donna sorrounded
by angels and the
twelve Apostles,
while below are the
groups of the
Blessed, on the left,
and the Damned, on
the right. The fresco
continues with the
cliffs, circles and pits
of Hell over Lucifer
towers, which is a
free pictorial
representation of
Dante's allegory.*

Hell a detail. - Rocks circles, "bolgia" with inscriptions; on the left side, the famous verse "You who enter, give up hope". In the centre dominates the terrible image of Lucifer biting Nebuchadnezzar, Julian the Apostate, Attila and others. Tangles of naked bodies and hairy demons complete the terrifying scene of the Dantesque Hell. The identity of the author of this painting is not certain. Through the centuries, however, it has been attributed to various artists. The contemporary critics attribute it to Francesco Traini.

The triumph of death, the Ladies of the Orchard -View of the flowered garden in which the princely group delights in pleasing conversation and sweet music that symbolize earthly joys.

STORIES OF ST. RANIERI

Among the most important pictorial cycles, together with the frescoes of the hall of the Triumph of Death, we find the Stories of St. Ranieri, the patron saint of Pisa, begun by Andrea Bonaiuti of Florence and, after his death, completed by Antonio Veneziano. Then there are the stories of the Holy Martyrs Efiso and Potito of Pisa, painted by Spinello Aretino, an artist who used a rapid technique and painted in a vivid and pleasant way, and lastly, the Stories of the Old Testament. They were begun by Piero di Puccio of Orvieto, who painted only the first three stories, and were completed, after long time, by Benozzo Gozzoli of the school of Ghiberti and the Blessed Angelico.

MUSEUM OF THE "SINOPIAS"

The problem of the conservation of the "Sinopias" (preparatory underdrawings in chalk) in the Camposanto (cemetery) of Pisa has been posed ever since 1947, when they came to light during the operation of removing the first of the frescoes superimposed over them from the wall. The "Sinopias" were then provisionally displayed partly on the walls of the Camposanto itself and partly in the rooms built behind the Camposanto's North side in 1952. Leading scholars then took part in the debate on the problem of their more permanent collocation which continued from 1963 to 1968 and which ended with the identification of a more suitable venue: namely, the rooms of the nearby Hospital of Santa Chiara (or Hospital of Pope Alexander IV, a brick building erected by

Giovanni di Simone in 1263). This was no longer being used as a hospital building, and the use of part of it facing onto the monumental complex was acquired by the Cathedral Works for museum purposes in 1969. The building occupies the greater part of the Piazza's longitudinal southern side. On the completion of the work of converting the premises, the Museum of the "Sinopias" was inaugurated in June 1979. An ingenious system of interconnecting walkways at different heights permits optimum viewing of the "Sinopias" which are displayed on two levels mounted on well-lit panels and accompanied by illustrative material, describing the methods of removing in frescoes from the walls, and the consolidation and remounting of the Sinopie themselves.

The "sinopia" of the Sacrifice after the flood. This fresco, with the stories of Cain and Abel, the Building of the Arch and the Landing of the Arch on Mt. Arata, is the last work realized by Piero di Puccio in the cycles of the Stories of the Old Testament.

Benozzo Gozzoli - The Annunciation (1470).
This fresco was painted in the Ammannati Chapel and set above the arch of the entrance. The discovery of the sinopias has been very useful in this case. The delicate image of the Angel who gives a lily to the Virgin and the moving figure of the Madonna designed under a particular inspiration are artistically speaking, much better than the fresco which covered it.

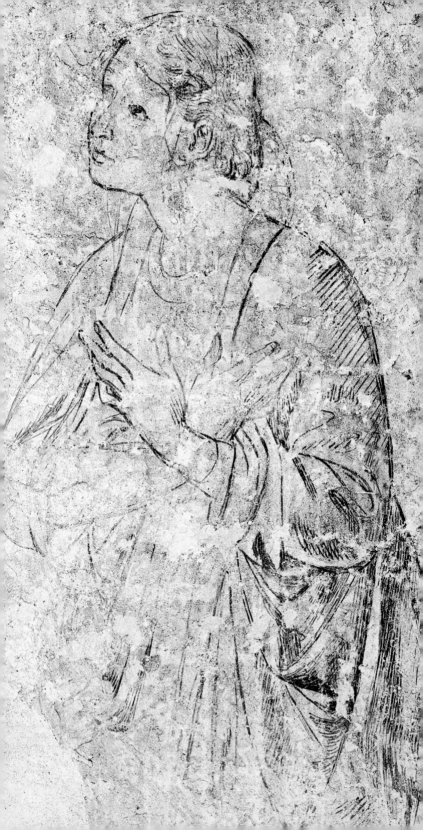

CATHEDRAL MUSEUM

The building which houses the Museum, an architectural complex situated at the eastern edge of the most beautiful lawn in the world, the Piazza dei Miracoli, consists of two wings grafted at right angles to a 13th century tower and enclosing a handsome cloister. From the 13th to the early 17th century it was the seat of the Cathedral Canons, and its present appearance dates to the latter period, when the diocesan Seminary was transferred here, where it remained throughout the 18th century Later it passed into private hands and became the residence in turn of the litterateur Giovanni Rosini and the Academy of Fine Arts. In 1887 it became the convent of the Capuchin nuns, from whom it was purchased by the Cathedral Works (Opera della Primaziale) in 1979. Following a complex and thorough restoration, it was then destined by the latter as the seat of the present Cathedral Museum. The works of art displayed in the Museum come from the monumental buidings on the Piazza dei Miracoli.

On the ground floor is situated the central nucleus of the Museum consisting of sculptures dating from the 11th to the 13th century. Among the early works are the Griffin, a rare Fatimid work, the Christ deposed from the Cross in polychrome wood by a Burgundian artist and the imposing series of sculptures by Rainaldo and Guglielmo from the façade of the Cathedral. We then come to the masterpieces of Nicola and Giovanni Pisano and Tino di Camaino: to the former two are dedicated three rooms and a side of the cloister with the busts and statues removed from the exterior of the Baptistery, the Madonna and Child known as the "Madonna del Colloquio" and the Madonna of Henry VII. The works of Tino di Camaino, the greatest Sienese sculptor of the 14th century, include the Altar - Tomb of St. Ranieri and the group of the Emperor Henry VII and his Counsellors. Datable to the second half

Wooden, Crucifix of the Burgundian school. According to tradition, it was brought by the Pisans from Bethlehem on the occasion of the First Crusade. Very well preserved, this is an extremely rare polychrome sculpture by unknown artist of the 12th-13th century.

of the 14th century are the Archbishops' tombs attributable to the workshop of Nino Pisano, while to the fully-developed Early Renaissance style belong the works of the Florentine sculptor Andrea Guardi, the sculptor of the Magnificent Ricci Tomb (c. 1455), Matteo Civitali, Staglo Stagi, Tribolo and Silvio Cosini. The most precious section of the Museum is concentrated in the rooms housing the Cathedral Treasury and the earliest surviving liturgical vestements. Here are displayed the famous ivory Madonna and Child and Crucifix by Giovanni Pisano: the red damask "Girdle" of the Cathedral decorated with enamelled plaques, gems and silver crosses: the Limoges reliquaries (12th-l3th century) and those France Maria de' Medici, wonderful examples of French goldsmith's work (1616-1617). On the first floor are displayed works of painting. Apart from an altar piece by a pupil of Benozzo Gozzoli (1470), the paintings date in the main from the 16th to the 18th century (including works by Battista Franco, Orazion Riminaldi, Aurello Lomi, Giuseppe and Francesco Melani and Giovan Battista Ferretti). Also on display are wooden sculptures by Giovan Battista Riminaldi. This is followed by fragments of the wooden choir-stalls from the Cathedral and liturgical manuscripts, including two splendid illuminated Exultet scrolls dating to the 12th and 13th century. Of considerable interest are the various examples of fabric and embroidery. These range from the 15th century Saddle-Cloth to the complete liturgical vestments of the 16th and 17th century; the various 18th century fabrics, mainly of French production, the specimens of lacework from Flander, and the imposing vestments of the 19th century.

Undoubtedly the most precious work in the Treasury is the ivory Madonna and Child of Giovanni Pisano. It originally stood on the High Altar of the Cathedral within a tabernacle placed over an altarpiece, it too in ivory, with scenes from the life of Christ. In this work which dates to 1299-1300, the sculptor was probably inspired by a French prototype, but some of its features are entirely novel and peculiar to Giovanni's own art, such as toe pronounced curvature reflecting that of the elephant tusk from which the figure was carved.

The Hyppogryph, a horse with the wings and beak of an eagle, which the. Pisan soldiers brought back home during the Crusades.

The beautiful and famous sculpture by Giovanni Pisano, representing the Madonna with the Child. The life which animates the works of this great artist reveals itself particularly in this simple Madonna, as a royal mother who, with pride and wonder, looks at her divine Son, on whose face the happy grace of childhood shines.

Henry VII of Luxemburg and his Counsellor, a work by the Sienese sculptor Tino di Camaino. This monument was erected by the Pisans to the memory of the unfortunate Emperor, who descended into Italy to be crowned in Rome. The hope of those who had been banisched and exiled, this sovereign strove to restore peace to the cities implacably pitted against each other in war, but died at the Battle of Buonconvento in August 1313. He is celebrated in Dante's Paradise.

Another beautiful Madonna with the Child. It is in the centre, among the statue of St. John the Baptist, all of the school of Nicola Pisano.

Two Limoges caskets decorated with historia ted scenes glorifying the theme of the Redemption.

Moses with the tables of the Law.

Madonna and Child.

The nine busts aligned in a row under the portico were removed in 1946 from the openings below the tympana on top of the external arcading of the Baptistery. They represent the Madonna and Child, the Four Evangelists with their symbols, Moses with the Tables of the Law, David with his harp, and two Prophets. The work of Nicola Pisano and his son Giovanni, they were probably sculpted between 1269 and 1279, when Giovanni moved to Siena to take in hand the façade of Siena Cathedral. Their compositional conception is perhaps attributable to Nicola, with the possible exception of the two Prophets which seem to be closer in style to the hand of Giovanni, who undoubtedly contributed to their sculptural realization. Imbued with a profound dramatic sense, which can still be felt today in spite of their corrosion, they represent the earliest and most striking attempts at monumental statuary made by the celebrated school of the Pisani.

THE TOWN OF PISA

The white monuments of Piazza dei Miracoli constitute undoubtedly the main attraction and the most significant element of the artistic patrimony of Pisa. And together with the famous Leaning Tower and the marble Cathedral, the magnificent frescoes of the Churchyard and the treasures kept in the Museum of St.

Matthew draw mainly the attention of the tourist.

It is not less interesting to discover the character of Pisa, in its streets and squares, in the promenade along the Arno, its houses and old churches.

Very near to the Piazza dei Miracoli, there is the 16th century Archbishop's House, with an ample portico, in whose centre there is a statue made by Vaccà, representing Moses. On the groudfloor of the house there are the archiepiscopal archives, where precious documents and parchments going back to the 8th century, are kept.

THE CHURCH OF ST. CATHERINE

The Church, erected by the Dominican Friars at the end of the 15th century, has an elegant Gothic portico and, on a side, beautiful belfry with mullioned windows, probably one of Giovanni di Simone's works.

The monocusped façade, unfortunately attached to civil buildings, is entirely made of marble. The interior, not always successfully restored after the 1651 fire, looks solemn, with one nave and with all the formerly existing sculptures.

The monumental tomb of Gherardo Compagni, on the right wall, is particularly interesting. A statue of the Pietà adorns the sarcophagus, a fine Pisan works of the end of the 14th century.

ST. ZENO

Not far away from St. Catherine's near the city walls, there is the ancient Benedectine Abbey of St. Zeno.

Already existing in the 10th century, the Abbey belonged to the Benedectines and later to the Camaldolites. The interior of the church, with three naves, keeps clearly the mark of the original construction completed between the 10th and 13th centuries. Because of its great archi-tectonic significance, the Abbey has been recently restored and so the beautiful façade, the interior and the portico have recovered their primitive beauty.

PIAZZA DEI CAVALIERI

The beautiful square, harmoniously enclosed by a noble architectonic structure of the 16th and 17th centuries, was the Elders'-Palace, which, when Pisa fell under the Medici, was transformed by Vasari, by order of Cosimo I. He made it the seat of the Order of the Knights of St. Stephen founded by him in order to defend the Tyrrhenian coast from the Muslim raids. The famous Aretine architect animated the simple façade of the building, which today houses the "Scuola Normale Superiore" (a College), founded in 1810 by Napoleon, with elegant graffito decorations and ogival niches containing busts of the Grand Dukes of Tuscany. The Palazzo dell'Orologio, now Gherardesca, closes the square. It was for the Order of the Knights of St.

Stephen in 1607. Vasari himself designed the building with great architectonic intuition, joining two separate buildings together by an arch, not to break the street. The two buildings are the "Torre delle Sette Vie" (The Tower of the Seven Streets) or Town Prison, and the remains of the Tower Prison, and the remains of the Tower of the Gualandi, called Tower of the Muda. It was in this tower that Count Ugolino della Gherardesca with his sons and nephews was imprisoned, until they starved to death. A marble stone commemorates that tragedy with some verses from the canto XXXIII of the Hell of Dante, one of the most moving and indignant passages of the Divine Comedy. The Tower of the Muda is also called the Tower of Hunger.

CHURCH OF ST. STEFANO DEI CAVALIERI

In the beautiful, harmonious square, on the right of the Palazzo dei Cavalieri or "della Carovana", there is the Church of St. Stephen. The church and the belfry of various styles were designed and built by Vasari in 1565-72. The simple marble façade, one of Don Giovanni de' Medici's works was erected between 1594 and 1606. On the sides of the façade there are two brick wings formerly the dressing-room of the Order, later transformed into naves. The interior has one nave with two wings.

The wooden ceiling, richly inlaid with gold, is very beautiful. In its panels there are paintings representing the "Deeds of the Knights". They are six paintings by Cristofaro Allori, Cigoli, Empoli and Ligozzi. Turkish trophies and flags, wooden sculptures which once adorned the ships of the Order, hang from the walls. Above, among the windows, you can see the lights of the ships. In the choir, behind the main altar, there is the golden bronze bust of St. Lussorio or Rossore, made by Donatello in 1427.

The wooden ceiling of the caisson realized in 1605, with the paintings of the "Deeds of the Knights" and one rich wooden sculpture which adorned the ships of the Order of St. Stephen, with trophies of Turkish flags.

Bust of St. Lussorio, by Donatello - Precious reliquary in gilt bronze that is found in the Church of St. Stephen.

THE UNIVERSITY

The town of Pisa, among its various cultural institutions, has one of the oldest universities in Italy. The Pisan University originated from a "Studio" existing since the 12th century, which was first organized by Count Fazio della Gherardesca, after he rose to power in 1328. Renewed and enlarged many times under the Medici, the University of Pisa had some of its faculties suppressed by the Gran Duke Leopold II of Lorraine, because they were considered too open to liberalism.

The University of "Sapienza" (Wisdom) has a very rich library, which keeps original documents of famous artists and scientists, among whom Galileo Galilei who studied and taught in this institute.

The 15th century building has a mediocre façade built in 1900, while the court-yard has an ample and elegant 16th century portico. On its back, a monument commemorates the heroic Resistance of the Pisan students at the battle of Curtatone in 1848. In the Main Hall there is the flag of the university students who fought on that occasion. Near the University there is the famous and characteristic 13th century "Torre del Campano" (Bell Tower), belonging to the University since the 18th century. Since that time, every morning, its bell tells the beginning of the lesson.

THE CHURCH OF ST. FREDIANO

Near the University, in a small square, there is the harmonious church of St. Frediano.
Founded by the Buzzacherini Sismondi family in the 11th century, it was renewed in the 16th and 17th centuries.
The simple Romanesque façade, with Pisan and Lucchese influences, has large pensile arches or resting on pilaster strips and, above, a large mullioned window.
The interior, restored after the 1675 fire, is very interesting.

It has three naves divided by Corinthian columns and Romanesque capitals.

THE CHURCH OF ST. FRANCIS

Walking along Via S. Francesco, in the homonymous square one meets the church of St. Francis, probably founded by some disciples of the saint in 1211 and completed by Giovanni di Si-

mone, between 1265 and 1270. The upper part of the simple façade, with white and grey marbles, was finished in 1603.

The interior, luminous and simple, has one nave and a transept; it is Egyptian-cross shaped, with a truss roof.

Beautiful paintings of artists of the time adorn the ten altars. In the second chapel, on the right side of the main altar, called Chapel of the Gherardesca, there are the bones of Count Ugolino and his sons and nephews, who died of hunger in the Tower of the Muda. On the left corner of the belfry, a masterpiece of engineering attributed to Giovanni di Simone. Two sides are inserted into the walls of the church, while the remaining part rests on two large corbels joined by an arch. From the vestry one can reach the beautiful 15th century cloister, with 40 arches above the tombstones of famous personages, among whom Francesco Buti, the first expounder of Dante.

SAN MICHELE IN BORGO

Garibaldi Square, which separates the Lungarno Pacinotti from the Lungarno Mediceo and faces the Ponte di Mezzo, is the centre of the city life. From pillars, with 11th - 17th centuries capitals. A little further on, on the left, among the houses, there is the Church of S. Michele in Borgo, an old church erected in 990, perhaps on the ruins of a pagan temple, with a beautiful marble façade of Romanesque - Pisan style, with decorations of Gothic style. It is one of the most harmonious works of Guglielmo Agnelli. Three Gothic portals, with a central niche and lunettes, complete the harmonious façade.

The simple interior, recently restored, is divided by imposing columns with various capitals.

At the first altar on the left, one can admire the beautiful marble Crucifix of the Pisan school of the 14th century. In the inside lunette of the left portal there is a 13th century fresco representing

St. Michael, which came to light furing the 1948 restorations.

Not far away there is the 16th century Piazza delle Vettovaglie, flanked with a beautiful portico. Since the 16th century, a market takes place in this square and even now it is one of the most characteristic and animated areas of old Pisa.

PONTE DI MEZZO

Situated in the centre of the town in order to link the most animated areas together, this bridge was first built by the Romans and till 1182 it was the only bridge on the Arno, in Pisa. In

1388 it was rebuilt by Pietro Gambacorti, probably because it was unsafe. Again in ruins, it was rebuilt by the architect Francesco Nave in 1660. The present bridge, with only one arcade, goes back to the post-war period. Recently the so called Game of the Bridge has been instituted again. It is a modern but spectacular version of an ancient and popular tourney going back to the beginning of the 15th century.

PALAZZO TOSCANELLI

In the centre of Lungarno Mediceo there is the Palazzo Toscanelli, once attributed to Michelangelo. It is the seat of the State Archives, which keep, among many Pisan documents, some preceding the first Crusade. During his stay in Tuscany in 1821, the famous poet George Byron lived in it for almost a year.

ROYAL PALACE

The Tower of The Golden Rod once belonging to the ancient Caetani family, this massive housetowers is also known because from it Galileo showed the first stars discovered by means of his spyglass, to the Grand Duke of Tuscany. The palace with which it forms a corner, with its beautiful façade on the Lungarno Pacinotti, is the Royal Palace. Built by Baccio Bandinelli in 1559 for Cosimo I de' Medici, the palace was later enlarged by putting other 14th century buildings together. It be-

came so the winter residence preferred by the Medici family. Renewed by the Lorena, mainly by Leopold II, the Royal Palace today houses the Superintendence of Monuments and Galleries.

THE AGOSTINI PALACE

Situated almost in of Ponte di Mezzo, the Agostini Palace is the only one which still remains of the typical Pisan brick-houses, adorned with sculptures and reliefs. Erected at the beginning of the 15th century, it has a beautiful façade with rich terracotta decorations. This palace is also known because it housed, during the period of the Italian "Risorgimento", the "Caffè dell'Ussero", a famous meeting place of patriots and university students, among whom many died in the battles of Curtatone and Montanara. The nearby "Via XXIX Maggio" (May 29th Street) reminds us of that date.

THE PALAZZO ALLA GIORNATA

This is the Palazzo Lanfreducci (later Uppezzinghi), but better known, due to the incomprehensible motto written on the architrave of its portal, as the "Palazzo alla Giornata". Designed by Cosimo Pugliani in c. 1600, it now houses a University Institute.

THE MEDICI PALACE

It is a beautiful building which looks like an elegant housetower, which is reflected in the Arno, adorning that wonderful stretch of the Lungarno Mediceo between the Ponte di Mezzo and the Ponte della Fortezza. The palace belonged to the Appiano family, which ruled in Pisa from 1392 to 1398. Since 1400 it belonged to the Medici. Laurence the Magnificent, too, lived in it. The main body, with three floors in white - grey stones, opens to the Lungar-

no with a beautiful portal. Fine mullioned, windows with elegant ogival, slightly trilobe lunettes lighten the façade. The palace is now the seat of the Prefecture.

THE CHURCH OF ST. MATTHEW

On the Lungarno Mediceo, just after the Medici Palace, there is the Church of St. Matthew, rebuilt between the 11th and the 13th centuries and partly restored in the 18th century.
On the side facing the Lungarno you can still see the original Romanesque arches. The belfry was lowered by the Florentines after the conquest of Pisa. In the interior, on the vault, you can admire "St. Matthew in the Heavenly Glory", by Francesco and Giuseppe Melani brothers. In the same square, attached to

the church, there is the entrance to the National Museum of St. Matthew.

NATIONAL MUSEUM OF ST. MATTHEW

Apart from the wonderful works of art in Piazza dei Miracoli, in Pisa there is one of the most important museum of Europe, namely the Pisan National Museum. In it we find sculptures and paintings of the Tuscan schools from the 13th to the 15th centuries and above all a good number of sculptures made by the great masters of the Pisan school, from Bonanno to Nicola, constitued by a group of paintings collected by Canon Zucchetti and donated by him to the Works Department of the Cathedral in 1796. The collection was enriched with successive donations and rearranged in 1893 in the former convent of St. Francis, where it remained till the last world war. The Museum is now situated in the old convent of the Benedictine Nuns of St. Matthew, on the Lungarno Mediceo. The architectonic set, much altered through the centuries in its original structure, has been completely restored after the war, so recovering its austere beauty. The halls are furnished with modern equipments in order to keep precious collections, which offer a complete and vast view of the development of the Pisan art.

The cloister of the Monastery is very suggestive with its green court-yard surrounded by mullioned windows, which have partly preserved their original 15th century look.

Right-hand page: Madonna del Latte, by Nino Pisano - Beautiful group whose delicate line is accented by the lively polychromy.

Saint Sebastian and St. Rocco by David Ghirlandaio.
Tempera painting on wood of the end of the 15th century.

On the side plate, the delicate and wonderful image of the Virgin in a painting by
Gentile of Fabriano.

THE FORTRESS, ALSO CALLED THE NEW CITADEL – SCOTTO GARDEN

Was built by the Florentines in 1468, but the Pisan destroyed it when they recover their freedom, even if it was for a brief period of time.

Having recaptured Pisa, the Florentines built the fortress again in 1512, on design of Giuliano da Sangallo having been damaged during the last world war, of this fortress there remain only some bastions, the glacies and the vaulted dungeons. The area between the Bastion of Sangallo and Palazzo Corsini, once Scotto, has been transformed into a beautiful public garden, with 18th century floral architecture.

THE CHURCH OF ST. PAUL ON THE ARNO

Built in 805, it was completely re-built during the 11th and 12th centuries and re-dedicated by Eugene III in 1148. The marble façade has grey-black stripes and a high tuff base.

The lower part has five blind arcades; the main portal is adorned with a precious, finely cut architrave.

The upper part of the façade has three orders of loggias.

The shapes of the arches and twisted columns already reveal a development of the Pisan art.

As the façade, the beautiful left side, too, repeats, in the successive high blind arcades, the main architectonic motif of the Cathedral.

The Egyptian cross-shaped interior has three naves with a transept, dome and semicircular apse.

The naves are divided by granite columns coming from the quarries of Elba, with interesting Romanesque capitals.

CHAPEL OF ST. AGATHA

Behind the church of St. Paul "a Ripa d'Arno" there is the Romanesque Chapel of St. Agatha, a brick building of the 12th century. The octagonal chapel is surmounted by an original pyramid - shaped dome. On five sides of the octagon, crowned by a harmonious cornice with small arches, there are elegant mullioned windows with high arcades. The interior, particularly simple, has, on the sides, arches shaped like a horse-shoe. Because of its structural similarities with the church of the Holy Sepulchre, it is probable that this chapel was designed by the architect Diotisalvi.

THE CHURCH OF THE HOLY SEPULCHRE

The architectonic structure of the small church of the holy Sepulchre is very suggestive with its slender, cuspidated dome and the nearby square belfry. As the inscription on the base of the belfry tells us, the church was built in 1153 by the architect Diotisalvi in order to keep the relics of the holy Sepulchre, here brought from Jerusalem. The church, made of grey stones, is octagonal with simple decorations inspired by the Holy Sepulchre. In the lunette of the portal facing the square, there is the bust of Diotisalvi, by Sante Varni. In the interior, eight pillars, on which ogive arches rest, support the elegant octagonal dome. At the foot of the altar, there is the tomb of Maria Mancini Colonna, a favourite of Louis XIV and niece of Cardinal Mazzarino. The beautiful Romanesque - Pisan belfry was begun, but not finished, by Diotisalvi.

GAMBACORTI PALACE

Now the Town Hall. - Among the most beautiful medieval houses of the town there is the Gambarotti Palace, built in the Gothic - Pisan style, in the 14th century. The façade divided into three orders by thin cornices, opens in the upper parts with high, elegant mullioned windows with marble Corinthian columns. Another thin cornice unites the arches wich include the small, trilobe arches of the windows, giving so a peculiar harmony to the severe stone façade.

The palace was built by Pietro Gambacorti, when he was in power. Gambacorti was murdered in 1393, just on the threshold of his house. Among the inside halls, that called "Baleari", on the first floor, now the Council Hall, is particularly noteworthy. Fine, allegorical frescoes of the 16th and 17th centuries, exalting the deeds of Pisa on the sea, adorn its walls.

SANTA MARIA DELLA SPINA

This small church, a charming Gothic building crowned by a delicate lace of pinnacles and niches, is situated on the Lungarno Gambacorti, at the Ponte Solferino. Originally it was an oratory dedicated to S. Maria di Pontenuovo and in 1323 took the present shape, when the main noble Pisan families, specially the Gualandi family, shared expenses. It was called "S. Maria della Spina" because a thorn (in Italian, "spina") of Christ's crown was kept there. In 1871 the church of S. Maria della Spina, which previously rose on the Arno, was disassembled and again completely assembled on the present Lungarno, because of dangerous seepage of water. The tricuspidal façade is crowned by tabernacles with statues representing the Redeemer and Angels, a fine work of the school of Nino Pisano.

The right side in particularly rich: the spires, the thirteen niches with the statues of the Apostle and, in the centre, the Redeemer, are all works of the school of Giovanni Pisano. In interior, on the left side of the altar, there is a small tabernacle, one of Staglo Stagi's works, which contained the relics of the Holy Thorn. The "Madonna del Latte" (Our Lady of the Milk), a masterpiece of Nino Pisano, and the "Cardinal and Theological Virtues", low-reliefs of the choir of Andrea di Francesco Guardi, have been transferred from this church to the National Museum. The altar was made by Cervellara in 1524.

THE FORTRESS OR OLD CITADEL

Two constructions characterize the Lungarno Simonelli.

The first one coming from the Lungarno Pacinotti, is the "Arsenale Mediceo" (Medicean Shipyard), called also "of the Galleys". It includes of the Order of St. Stephen On the outside walls you can read some inscriptions commemorating the naval victories of the Order and recording the number of the galleys which took part in the exploits, the number of the Christians who were freed and of the prisoners.

A little further, stretched out on the river, there rises the Fortress or Old Citadel. The ancient fortress was re-built and enlarged by the Florentine soon after the conquest of the town in 1405.

The beautiful Guelph Tower has been completely re-built, having suffered great damages during the last war. During the restoration of the 15th century building which closes the ancient ground gate of the Pisan shipyard, a drawbridge gate has come to light with it. Other interesting discoveries have taken place in the area where the 13th century Pisan Shipyard was.

It is pleasant, in quiet evenings, to enjoy the sunset, walking along the Pisan "Lungarni". The illuminations, however, on June 16th, on the occasion of St. Ranieri's Feast, are simply fantastic Here are the Lungarno Mediceo and Lungarno Galilei with numberless lights, reflected in the slow waters of the Arno, mingling with the last blazing lights of the day.

The traditional city festivals, which go back to many centuries ago, generally take place in the month of June. First of all, we mention the feast in honor of St. Ranieri, the patron saint of the town, which begins on June 16th, in the evening, with fantastic illuminations on the Lungarnos, followed by spectacular fire works. Following a usage going back to 1300, the windows of all the houses and the parapets of the Lungarnos are adorned with candles and oil - lamps, while on the Arno numberless floating torches, called "Lampanini", go slowly towards the sea. On the next day the Historical Regatta of St. Ranieri takes place on the Arno. The crews of the quarters of Sant'Antonio, San Francesco, Santa Maria and San Martino, in their traditional costumes and in ancient boats, take part in it. Since June 1956, the Regatta of the Ancient Seafaring Republics, which takes place every year alternatively in one of the four towns Amalfi, Genoa, Pisa and Venice, has been added to the traditional festivals of the "Pisan June". The Regatta, with crews in costumes and on ancient boats, is preceded by a magnificent and picturesque Historical Parade. Among the various personages, surrounded by warriors, captains, damsels and pages, in their precious costumes made on designs of the time, you can notice Kinzica de'Sismondi, the popular heroine who, according to a tradition, by her courage saved the town of Pisa from a fire set by the Saracens; then the Duke of Amalfi with a magnificient golden costume, the Genoese Guglielmo Embriaco, called "Testa di Maglio", the Doge of Venice and Caterina Cornaro.

The Game of the Bridge is another folk event which takes place on the first Sunday of June. In

this very old game, the two parties of the "Tramontana" and "Mezzogiorno", representing respectively the quarters to the North and South of the Arno, try to push, using all their strenght and astuteness, a beavy cart sliding on rails, situated in the centre of the Ponte di Mezzo. The prize, the "Palio", will be given to the winning party on the following Sunday in the Town Hall. This ceremony will be followed by various celebrations and illuminations in the districts of the winning party. The Game of the Bridge is also an interesting historical commemoration, in which many citizens take part in their rich costumes.

OUR WARMEST THANKS:

To the Pisa Tourist Board for the kind concession of the
city map and the drawing of Leaning Tower.

Text: Roberto Donati
Photos: Archivio Plurigraf - Ag. Stradella -
The Image Bank - Atlantide - Sie - Marka -
Il Dagherrotipo - Fabrizio Sbrana - Laura Ronchi.